LINDA D. ADDISON
ALESSANDRO MANZETTI

THE PLACE OF
BROKEN
THINGS

Let the world know:
#IGotMyCLPBook!

Crystal Lake Publishing
www.CrystalLakePub.com

Readers will inherit
the world

SUMMARY

THE DEAD DANCER

by Linda D. Addison & Alessandro Manzetti

At first, when she started dancing,
at the same time each day,
(wearing a grotesque black and white suit)
the walls of the purple room seem
to shine, opening warm crevices, new windows
without an outside or a landscape out there,
as if the bricks are guided by the second movement
of Tchaikovsky' Pathétique, a transparent absinthe,
maybe waiting for the golden eggs of love
to bloom inside their old beams;
a false hope repeating infinitely.
—can loneliness have a soundtrack?—

But then, drums explode suddenly,
at the same time each day,
(and you can hear the horns mourning)
making the music change, blowing storm,
letting the dancer become aware,
with eyes as big as underworld's coins,
of the pallor of her own skin and
the wet cold of that abandoned house,
the vanishing scene of something bad,
the dance floor of eternal return;
a false face, a flesh mask mirroring the past.
—can we die again and again, so many times?—

Her back bent, dreams become strings
played by Tchaikovsky' Pathétique, hope &
tears promised by Movement Three, dancing for
you more than once, (can we die more than
once?) and waltz endless on legs stretched
into the earth, mouth extending into horn
sections, moving without making a sound.
Did you see it, when the walls bled as an
invisible conductor spun light full of shadow?
—can denial become an endless meal?—

Allegro molto vivace, roaring softer,
softer in the mind, reaching the locked door,
the too small window, until toes melt, legs
freeze in place, gaze held in place, golden
threads seducing all ghosts, reminding us
what grace can end, what grace can begin,
will never be enough to extinguish the
small flame, the wheel going no where.
—can the moth escape the glass bell?—

KOLKATA'S LITTLE GIRL

by Alessandro Manzetti

Upper Street, at midday.
Bandhura is counting the yellow cabs
go back and forth
with their human heads
sticking out from the car doors.
She's waiting, in front of a blue-clothes shop
for someone to tell her story;
It's only five rupees.
—fifty-two, fifty-three

She's only eight,
a too long and heavy necklace
hanging around her orange neck;
a strange rosary, with its
amethyst crystal's purple beads.
She's still waiting, with her
shining so ancient eyes,
those of a homeless angel
with a pearl piercing her tongue.
—seventy-five, seventy-six

A Thai boy, with a toothy smile
and bright yellow flip-flops
stops near her; he seems to smell the air.
Maybe he notices me? thinks Bandhura.
Or did he catch her scent?

But the boy lifts his fancy camera and
takes a picture of a reddish rickshaw
caught in a massive traffic jam,
and then disappears, without a glance.
—eighty-five, eighty-six

It's only five rupees, Sir
whispers the little girl, stretching her hand
towards a tall English gentlemen
wearing a Colonial suit at least a century older
walking past her piece of sidewalk,
her wicked place.
But he doesn't answer her,
holds a faded cigar in his teeth
like it's a piece of flavouring hope,
and continues on his way
skipping through stones and lives, like a little boy.
Maybe he's a ghost too, thinks Bandhura.
—one, two.

PHILLY'S LITTLE BOY

by Linda D. Addison

Inspired by Alessandro Manzetti's *Kolkata's Little Girl*

Chestnut Street, at midday.
Tommy is counting the yellow cabs
go back and forth, full of tourists
with their faces framed in windows.
He's waiting, in front of the manicured
park for someone to tell his story;
it's only one dollar.
—fifty-two, fifty-three.

He's only eight,
a thick leather collar around his golden
brown neck; a frayed rope hanging from
a loop at his throat; a strange rosary
for a thin boy. He's still waiting,
with eyes unblinking, so ancient, a
brand unhealed on his shoulder.
—seventy-five, seventy-six

A dark brown girl, with a toothy smile
and flowered yellow dress
stops near him; she seems to see him.
Maybe she notices me? thinks Tommy.
Or did she catch his shadow?
But the girl raises her hand and

waves to a man near him, who rushes
to lift her in his arms and run across
the busy street, without a glance at him.
—eighty-five, eighty-six

It's only one dollar, Ma'am
whispers the little boy, stretching his hand
towards a tall pale woman wearing a long
blue striped dress, a style at least a century older,
her blond hair piled high on her head, walking
past his piece of sidewalk,
this wicked place.
But she doesn't answer him, opens a lace parasol,
like it will deliver savory hope, and continues
on her way, skipping like a little girl.
Maybe she's a ghost too, thinks Tommy.
—one, two.

LIKE JAPANESE SILK

by Linda D. Addison & Alessandro Manzetti

Why are bells ringing at this time of night?
I wake with two crazy diamonds
embedded in my eye sockets.
I don't need to turn on the light,
I can find my way following the
shining red stripe (blood?) dripping
on the floor, toward the staircase
coiled like a watch spring.

Why are bells ringing at this time of night?
Maybe I already know the answer,
it must be the strange curse of this new
home, the only one in these hills
with a direct view of the church,
over there, in the middle of nowhere;
a bronze cross above the faded roof,
—which looks like the God's antenna—
of the old romanic building.

They told me to be careful
when I got here, like an apocalyptic pilgrim
without faith, without a wife,
no longer myself, after seeing
—It was Monday night, one year ago—

all that blood sprayed on asphalt,
the extravagant, surreal sculptures of
twisted metal and crude bones,
and her face—*look homeward, angel*
surprised to be dead.

I follow my red stripe, straight downstairs,
feeling no pain; whose blood is that?
There should be a wounded giant around here,
or maybe my crazy diamonds, my brand new eyes
don't work very well, and I'm seeing through
the misleading prisms of heroin,
my brand new wife—*an unfound door.*

I feel the grass between my toes
and the garden, the green tongue of my house,
seems to move each leaf, stones and roots
building a border for the little red river
which is pointing toward the Church
with its so smooth back, like Japanese silk.
Why am I walking outside at this time of night?
I should be asleep, my crazy eyes hidden
behind the shroud of strange love from my
reborn doctrine, in the stone arms of heroin.
Instead I step softly, following this flow of
scarlet, the full moon dancing on its maddening
surface—her eyes, craters trailing me.

Why am I walking outside at this time of night?
The bells still echoing—*bring out your dead,*
moonlight revealing/hiding the Church as clouds
dance overhead—I ignored the warnings, hungry

to forget a year ago, on my knees, my old eyes
staring at her ruby lips, one last time. Am I the
strange curse, stumbling back to the resting place?

Why aren't the bells ringing as I kneel at the edge
of the Church entrance? The rubicund path ends
here, leaving my palms dripping, my eyes hollow—
still I can see that I can not leave, the bronze cross
waits patiently for my confession, like Japanese silk.

IF YOU REMEMBER ME

by Linda D. Addison

Inspired by *If You Forget Me* by Pablo Neruda

They will allow you to know
one thing . . . *not the many things*
that were me.

You know how *they are*:
if they let you look
thru the glass window, at the red straps
holding me to the crystal table,
when they start the fire,
the infinite cracks
in my body, broken by the log,
everything of me will be carried away,
as if only *they* exist,
laughter, tears, caresses,
became little boats
that sail
toward *their* cold, locked isle.

Well, tomorrow,
when little by little you stop thinking of me
I shall stop being, little by little.

If suddenly
you can not recall me,
do not ask *them*,
for I shall already have been erased.

If you think this all madness,
let the wind of time
that passes through all lives,
become your decision,
leave me at the shore
of your distant heart where they chained me,
remember not
that last day,
that last hour,
lifting my head
so my mind was replaced
by another life.

But
if any day,
any hour,
you feel destined for
impossible joyfulness,
if each morning a thought
climbs down from your mind, seeking me,
ah my love, my fading hope,
in your mind *they* will find the fire,
in your thoughts all will be extinguished or erased,
your love will feed *their* ashes, beloved,
but as long as you live without me in your mind,
they can not break you.

JOY

by Alessandro Manzetti

Inspired by the movie *Joy*, written and directed by Sudabeh Mortezai

Joy shows her golden hands
to the winter sky; it's her special voodoo
to recognize demons and sordid Prince Charmings
and to survive another night, there
in her place on that street
full of Nigeria's jewels, black stripes of Youth,
while a half-woman and half-snake Lamia,
masked as a kitsch lady dressed in orange,
is waiting in a comfortable Mercedes
munching Chinese food.

Joy is under the protection of a warlock,
a fat man who lives in a shack, near a water well,
slaughtering hens, painting his body red
and spitting spells on walls for money.
She can hear his voice, his sadist mumbling
even thousands of miles away
—Pay Your debt!—
while a car is approaching her
with the windows open, and the ghost of Coltrane
in the passenger seat.

—Hey, precious—
The yellowish face of the man looks like
the mask of the future, without eyes,
without joy, and a golden tooth
shining, reflecting the North Star
half hidden by a rubber Himalaya
mountain of old tires, stacked in the
dump behind her, fenced with rows of
woven beads, what was left, still coloured,
the last squadron of embarked hopes.

Joy shakes her green bracelets,
improvising a dance, then her beautiful shape,
licked by the white, luminescent tongue of a lamppost,
lying down on the back seat, moves like a sacred snake
whispering to the stars, and far away things.
Now she's coiled around the equator,
a thousand miles away, no longer there.

But, suddenly, she gets nosebleeds,
something too real—*she's real*
something intolerable in that place,
in that row of exquisite empty bodies
and rosy crucifixions.

CITY WALKERS

by Linda D. Addison & Alessandro Manzetti

A pack of shaded neon eyes,
    promising sudden & savage feast,
    impenetrable things pace back & forth,
    obsessively licking their lips,
waiting for the first drop of fear.

Like tigers, escaped from the Borges
    imaginary regions of Tlön and Mlejnas with
    their collars made of pieces of Asian mirrors,
    obsessively reflecting faces, prey,
waiting to catch your smell.

Alpha recognizing the weak link, invites
    you to the golden fields to become the
    unseen, the denied things needing destruction,
    endlessly walking in circles, work/home/work . . .
tripping all others waiting for recognition.

It has a circle tail, like an ouroboros,
    it's blind, like anything else newborn,
    and hides in its cosmic belly eggs of nothing,
    close to hatching & breathes another dimension
detected by human eyes.

Omega looking to defuse clarity, switches
    places with the meal, for a second, unfairly
    playing hope, like an on/off game, then
    stepping back with a howl,
leaving you in the center again, waiting.

With its dark fur and worn fangs, observes
    getting closer its muzzle, flying flock of days,
    crazy flies colliding all over each other, for years
    inside the upside-down glass of life,
looking for a crack, to escape the endless waiting.

SHE, ON SUNDAY

by *Alessandro Manzetti*

The ghost of Aysedeniz plays the piano
for its hundredth spring, moving cold fingers,
pressing blurry fingerprints on the ivory keys,
bleeding curves, lines and black and white mazes
which vibrate following the coils of a music theme,
only four chords repeating.
—all her remembrances when she was a young girl.

That day is resonating, repeating itself
through the yellowish plasma of the past,
in front of the sad smile of Istanbul.
She, popped out of the stone portholes
of the Galata Tower, is still breathing
that seventy three yards high clean air.
—a gasoline taste in her mouth, thinking she can fly.

The ghost of Aysedeniz plays the piano
for the thousandth time, maybe more
it's impossible to say, there, underground
in a so white room, without even a window
or something alive to pick, to bite, to grab:
a blackberry blush, a warm hand, or the slimy tail
of that moment escaped into its lair.
—always the same music, only four chords repeating.

That day is living again, repeating itself
she and that place glued together,
in front of the watery highway of the Bosphorus,
with its bridges and long fingers
attached on the edges of two continents.
The Turkish girl, dressed in black, a red rose between the
legs,
is still breathing, facedown
whispering a strange rosary, always the same words
—why me? why now? why in that place?

The ghost of AyseDeniz continue to play
the minimalist notes of Yann Tiersen;
they're so easy to understand, to follow,
like women's scents in the days
when the incense of spring begins to burn
attracting molecules of life
and sleeper crocodiles, with fancy hats,
ready to pick, to bite, to grab
what isn't theirs. She, on Sunday,
assaulted into the sacristy of a little church,
that smelled of wine and dead flowers.

That place.
—an interrupted blossoming, only four chords repeating.

A HYMN TO THE NIGHT

by Linda D. Addison

Inspired by Phillis Wheatley's *An Hymn to the Morning*

At the end of my day, after nine hours of work,
without help, soul weary of toiling as well as I can;
In my rough hands, a pen pours words onto paper,
for shadowy Nyx, child of Chaos, now demands
my prose. Nyx rides the mists of night, and all the
millions sleep. Which path do you progress through the
dim skies? Night falls, extends her hazy blanket over every
roof top & field the gentle breeze dances.

Disharmony waits for the sleeping to commence,
entering closed minds, shaking curtained windows.
Those shady workers gloom left behind office doors, to
shove this poet from their blistering day.

The Chief of all Muses arouses the hidden pain,
which injustice feeds to relentless fire:
the deadlines, the neon lights, the fevered hours,
all their pain in my battling soul. See in the west
the retreating king of day! His setting light
allowing Nyx deepest shadows entry—

But Oh! I feel her moon pull too strongly,
and begin my end-of-all-time prose.

WHILE THE ROOFTOPS BECOME RED

by Linda D. Addison & Alessandro Manzetti

Hush, she says,
while the red bulbs of Shanghai
are showing her breasts and thorns
(my mouth disappears)
and just behind her thin shape
a curve, an angle, a twisted strip
of the empty skin of Huangpu river
(no boats and barges, no living things)
like it was an eternal Sunday.

Hush, she says,
while the rooftops become red
like her necklace, her throat
(my hands disappear)
and just behind me, over by the window
the Oriental Pearl Tower, the antenna of the future
seems always the same, with its big orbs,
and so are the temples, the neons, the sleeping
steel numbered whales in the harbour,
as if she was still alive.

Hush, she says,
while red tears burn my chest,
a whisper in my ears, *I am the hunger*
(my legs disappear)
and just behind her walls of

the City God Temple shimmer
in the cooling pool of past
clients contaminating the
gardens of frozen Yulan magnolia
seeds stolen from dying dreams.

H-U-S-H, she carves
on my chest (with my hands),
the curved knife scraping my ribs,
while the rooftop burns, red rains
from the ceiling, and just behind me
a whisper, *you are the animal*
(my eyes disappear), before my last
breath I remember the old city walls
of Shanghai, where I found her, and
the knife, and the hunger . . . hush, she says
(my head disappears)

ANIMATION

by Linda D. Addison

When
it started
is lost in history. At work
a scream made me jump. Lights
flickered, the sound of concrete grating
behind walls. I ran to the middle
of the hallway as holes
crack open in
the walls.
Join us.

Deep
grating voices
whisper through holes,
walls crumble, twisted metal,
wires wiggle to the floor, then flow up
into a human shape: a head,
mouth, spiraling wire
arms reach out.
Join us.

Running to the exit stairway, I stumbled down
undulating steps, their mesh interior
moaning, louder, louder . . .
above a metal angel
descends.

Flesh body knitted with steel, eyes empty,
weeping blood floats in front of me.
Wire caresses my face,
enters my ears,
metal loops
bind me
to the
walls,
sweet static
blooms in my brain
singing the
way out.
Join . . .

AFTER THE ORDEAL

by Alessandro Manzetti

No one understands, no one can see
—not even watchers of the skies—
what I'm dragging now, like it was tons,
what put its hooks inside me,
revealing the truth of the black spaces,
the other side of the Moon, the slim bacon
of short seconds, and the block of grease
—the tasteless, sacred whale—
of fifty years of life spent on this planet.
Did you ever meet the Master of Pain?
It plays the guitar like Jimi Hendrix.

No one understands, no one can feel
—not even a disillusioned poet—
the barking inside me, the steel jaw traps
simultaneously snapped on my flesh,
a new mine camp with only one enemy.
Who am I? A psychedelic pinball
with sparkly bridges and steep ramps,
and a grenade rolling on my belly
tattooed with the mouth of Mary Magdalene?
Did you ever see the Master of Pain?
It likes the same brand of beer as Bukowski.

No one understands, no one can listen to
—not even a merciful gravedigger—
the steps of something without legs
which crawls below the soul's pagoda
scratching all your windows,
running like a surreal spheric hippo
between the infinite crash of crystal jewelry
inside the narrow alleys of the little I know,
until to the great splash in the pool of
my liquefied memories, seasoning my broth.
Are you the Master of Pain?
If so, sheriff, you should've killed me with your silver
bullets.

Hope no one has been the guest,
the first course, a duck in orange sauce,
as it happened to me, naked like the morning star
entangled in a too yellow sky,
imprisoned, chained to the wall
—the mosaic of myself, millions of pieces—
waiting for the Master of Pain,
with its Monday's mask
—an Henry Miller's rubber face—
and then walking on these streets
TRIESTE or TIMBUCTU' or CALCUTTA
after the ordeal.

OBSERVING THE FRAGMENTED

by Linda D. Addison & Alessandro Manzetti

theyze
    watched the life forms
on the blue, green planet
    through their viewers, perceiving only
    ranges of light, shades of colors
mesmerized by the destruction
    of body, soul, mind
    of land, water, air
by some beings reflecting much shadow
    violence denied
by some beings seeping grey thru colors
    restorative light magnified
 by some beings breathing in bloody shards.

theyze
    saw huge concrete cylinders, weird structures
and a green explosion in the East quadrant
    blinding their viewers, for a moment
    by the fingers of radioactive beings
rising from the destruction
    beings made of venom,
    licking the sky with their ionized tongues,
birthed by a shining, fat mother,
    an upside down shelled star, forming
    a new kind of silence
a perimeter of death magnified by grey rainbows
    making the observers change course.

FACING OLYMPIA

by Alessandro Manzetti

Some say you're held
in solitary confinement, for years,
on a Museum's white wall,
—Naked, right beside the Seine—
but I first saw you, voiceless odalisque,
near the gardens of the outskirts
of my imaginary town at midnight.
You looked like the goddess of waste
—A light bulb in the dark—
with your red leather suit
shining, a red reflecting surface
full of captured things;
eyes, tongues, nearly killed stars, moths.
—all the pieces of frustrated lives—

Others say you're only a painting
and know your real name;
—Venus, Olympia, Maja—
bullshit, you're flesh and blood like me,
like all the miserables entangled here
in the same streets, alleys,
in the same midnight,
always looking over their shoulder
—The pimp knows well how to use a knife—
always looking at you, at the same time,
from the car windows.
—She can turn a rat into a king—

Still others say you're a hooker,
naughty and too white skinned,
—Fifty bucks? Are you real?—
or an Orient ghost who has lost its way,
who feeds on the juice of men to survive.
—A beautiful kind of pain and abyss—
But it doesn't matter, I'll be dead
without finding you, each midnight,
here, in the midland of life
—Squeezed, lonely oranges—
where nothing else matters than
finding something familiar, beautiful
during the Alzheimer' tides.

HI HOOL

by Linda D. Addison

Inspired by *Writer's Coffeehouse Tucson*

a tree without roots
choked by windowless walls
my last thought is *you*

un albero senza radici
soffocato da muri senza finestre
il mio ultimo pensiero sei *tu*

mti bila mizizi
imechomwa na kuta zisizo na dirisha
mawazo yangu ya mwisho ni *wewe*

un arbol sin raices
asfixiado por paredes sin ventanas
mi último pensamiento eres *tu*

arboris radices non
constrictam windowless muros
tu tandem mei haec ita

A CLOCKWORK LEMON RESUCKED

by *Linda D. Addison & Alessandro Manzetti*

What's it going to be then, eh?
I was a poet, I was insane,
I was the radioactive milk, a virus
with green head and long tentacles.
I had never used black BMW,
a spaceship, a time machine
and it was so good to walk with Keats,
Blake, Ginsberg or old Hank
along the river.

I could hold a star in my hand
—Which one? You choose—
and, you wouldn't believe it,
I knew the secret of Mona Lisa,
and where loneliness was hidden.
My soul was yellow like a lemon,
like a Van Gogh's sunflower,
like the birthday of a free man.

I was a poet, I had golden teeth
and a cure for sorrow.
But now I look at the world from my cell window,
—Overlooking a dump and two lemon trees—
waiting for the last day of my reeducation,
locked in here, like a miniature of myself,
like a Cézanne painting in black and white,

with robotic maggots inside my brain.
I hate you Fortress, I hate you killers
of dreamers.

I could create a universe in my head
—Which? One you've never seen—
and you would believe it. I knew
the secrets of Mozart & Stevie Wonder,
where delicious madness was hidden.
My soul was bright like sunshine,
like fast fingers on a keyboard,
like daydreams of freedom.

I was a poet, I was a dreamer,
a cure for despair.
Soon I will look at the world from my cell window,
—Overlooking a dump and two lemon trees—
and become a creator of nothing, no opinions,
no songs, my mind sliced away by nano-mag-gots
so you can be safe & untouched. I will become
re-made into a collector of trash, silent & dulled.
I will not be able to hate, love, cry . . .
What's it going to be then, eh?

WHAT WE HAVE BECOME

by Linda D. Addison

What is this
   thing you became?
   With walls of white smoke
   & cracked mirrored windows
nailed shut with truth.

I fear some fleeting sanity,
   some sticky chaos
   in the endless story whispering
from glowing blue roses climbing
   impossible glass fences.

What is that
   thing they call you?
   With strange shadow cutouts dancing
   & soft flashing music
screaming secrets & lies.

I fear some denied desire,
   some crackling guilt
   in the nightmares mumbling
from dim blue light pouring down
   impossible glass staircase.

How have you tangled time & space
  in a knot with your tongue,
  recreating yourself & the world?
  Why am I the only one
who remembers Before . . .

MORNING STAR

by Alessandro Manzetti

So strange
feeling your flavor,
like a peel of prune on my tongue;
what am I experiencing?
I don't know,
but I like your new amaranth suit
and the sky's peace you brought here.

Entangled in this Victorian tower
—an angel's launching pad—
staring at you from a distance,
my beautiful Moore's living sculpture,
seeing the white wall
through the hole on your belly.

So strange,
feeling myself satisfied this way
—your flesh is black magic—
after so many years spent
in collecting new skin,
without wanting more
than wrappers of men and women
without touching anything, inside.
—I don't have my own shape, like you—

So strange,
feeling the scars on my back burning
and loving you just now,
dead, strangled, declaiming my name:
Morning Star.
—I'm what you want, each time—
You knew everything about me
but you didn't leave.
So strange.

THE PLACE OF BROKEN THINGS

by *Linda D. Addison & Alessandro Manzetti*

. . . constructed between echoing gasps
of pain, of twisted metal
in the moment before waking
the declining wisps of false dreams,
on the edges of ragged hope,
a so early abandoned love.

. . . constructed with the grey bricks
of absence, of imaginary presence
in the moment before sleeping,
the noise of the bumper cars of thoughts,
on the edges of a blurry place,
vanished long times ago.

. . . constructed between ancient scents
of shaving lotion, of sweet hairspray
before they smashed their heads
through the hungry windshield
on the edges of a road
forgotten by guardian angels.
. . . broken promise to be home early
while the child sleeps, without fear
one last gift to buy, one last breath taken,
orphaned by good intention, by chaos
slipping fragments of that day, into her soul
disfiguring childhood dreams.

. . . broken on Saturday, like the neck
of the blue-eyed Jenny the doll
right after the scream of brakes
in the moment before, to see
that place sweating red venom,
secretions of the unpredictable.

. . . frozen forever, there
with deflated yellow flowers around a photo
of dead smiles, and so white teeth
in front of a home, an unfound door
full of Christmas ornaments
shining red like their last curve on the road.

. . . frozen in the open wound of her heart
each time she drives to work
pass that hook in the road, the silence
echoing imagined screams, crunched bone,
brains discarded among wrapped gifts,
that one last gift—that Place.

SONG OF SOFT SPIRITS

by Alessandro Manzetti

Reworking of the poem *Go into the Highways and Hedges, And Compel Them to Come In* by Aleister Crowley

Closing the door, sealing the deal with
the loose aroma of the street
all over me, now (a second skin)
showing me the imaginary rich brown globes
of its sacramental meat.

I'm an old snake, I'm a purple lizard,
I'm a singing demon drunk on tequila,
golden wine and bright-eyed passerby;
I wear the Gide's glasses,
so I can measure height and weight
of joy and beauty, and recognize
the bright scent of intact young bodies.
(let me be your formaldehyde, your eternity)

Closing the door, sealing the deal with
a God of flesh and its little, spiced sons,
tasting them, in the distance,
with my prehistoric senses.
(it's more pleasant than at dawn to steal)

I'm the only reptile, here, in my divine home
(a nest of rats, near the church)
in this popular neighborhood, so flavored
by humanity, vanilla and dirty feet.
Let me taste you, living perfume,
while I change skin (look this green diamonds)
and listen to my new song
of soft spirits into rapture peal.

CATHEDRAL LANE

by Linda D. Addison

Waking, but keeping his eyes
closed, the sound of seagulls
make him smile, the scent of
salt water courses through his
body as he stretches on his king
sized bed, cardboard laid out
behind the dumpster of the
electronics store. Somewhere
in the distance the sun returns,
sliding up from the horizon, as
night retires he opens his eyes
to greet the passing of Now
from one sky god to another,
welcoming Nandzgai, His light
pouring red on the tops of the tall
buildings, bowing to Chahalgel as
the god of nightfall retreats, melting
in the glow of his brother. The hard
sounds of trash trucks making their
rounds interrupts his morning invocations.
It doesn't matter which day it is, except for
once a week when they invade his piece of
Earth to empty the dumpster, but that isn't
this day. He takes time to fold the cardboard,
roll up the blanket, tie it to his backpack and
walk slowly out of the canyon of alleys, step

carefully onto the concrete sidewalk, filling with
the river of people flowing into office buildings.
Standing in line at the coffee wagon, the woman
hands him a buttered roll, large coffee, he gives
coins from his pocket and walks away, she says,
"Have a good day, Chief."
He whispers, "I am no
naat'áanii, just a lost warrior", makes his way to
The Battery to sit & watch seagulls follow
boats, eat his roll and wonder
when
the
tribe
would
return
to take him home . . .

AND WHEN NO ONE IS WATCHING, NO ONE CARES

by Linda D. Addison & Alessandro Manzetti

Born when the first chewed apple
was dropped in the Garden,
transparent entrances open in the shadows
of trash-filled alleys, unlit closets,
under the beds of those who cry in their sleep.

In the beginning: it was silent, infinitely empty
except for one rotting apple core,
then came the new born calf with a deformed
hoof, waves of blood raining from its cut throat,
sacrificed by self-identifying enthusiasts.

All that blood, shining on obsidian blades
empowering it with the white electricity
of a cluster of stars, making its long, thin shadow
crawl up the walls, twist around pipes and necks,
shaking its ivory rattles, the music of longing.

It smells like honey, almonds and desolate rooms,
it can take human form, to pull you into its embrace.
A fake Janis Joplin appears in the alley, with a snake
tongue
and a syringe in one hand, dancing and whispering
in your ears: "Remember when you were young".

And you gyrate to her songs delivered to your
hungry veins, even when they break your heart,
even as your bones become dust in the space
of her breath. No one watches the transformation
of hope into nothing.

In the end: it is filled with the echo of backs turned,
moaning voices denying recognition to each thing
carelessly vomited from tightening throats, until
the day they crawl backwards out of random graves
to ask "Why?"

MUSEUM OF MISLEADING DIVERSIONS

by Linda D. Addison

Reincarnated 17 times, each key doesn't fit,
the door remains timeless, made of dark flowing
dreams, desire unspoken, at first glance presenting
as ebony wood, when stared at obscene movement
repels even wandering insane people.

Reading the sign 17 times, each instance a different
language, not deciphered, made of red glowing
liquid, wounds unhealed, at first glance presenting
as living flesh, when stared at creates dizziness
even in the most educated people.

Waiting for 17 days, the door opens, closing behind
a persistent seeker, who follows gold arrows floating
in the darkness, a low hum beckons, the air becomes
bitter steam, one step forward, the floor softens,
melts, swallowing the visitor without a sound.

Reincarnated 18 times, no key will ever fit,
the door is timeless, made of dark flowing
flesh, questions unspoken, at every glance
presenting as shadow play, when touched, skin
burns, peels, pulling even sane wanderers in . . .

COME ON YOU PAINTER, YOU PIPER, YOU PRISONER

by Alessandro Manzetti

Waiting for you, my crazy brother
(with a paintbrush and all the reds of Modigliani)
here, in this place called Asylum,
in this garden of gruesome delights.

Come on you painter, mosquito's voice
(find the way out through my ear)
show yourself, I have only an hour of air,
but miles of rope and tons of rotten dreams.

Come on you piper, sticky blues
(change music, how about Janis Joplin?)
look at those walking in circles around the fountain;
they're waiting for a new song, to reverse direction.

Come on you prisoner, leech roommate
(you got fried by the last electroshock treatment?)
I'll lend you a face, a bed, a half-hour of air,
I can't wait any longer, before using my ropes,
strangling our crazy marriage.

ALL, NOTHING, SOMETHING IN BETWEEN

by Linda D. Addison & Alessandro Manzetti

All
the theory of every thing,
a grazing unicorn, single horn radiating light
the echo of rustling in a shadowed woods
memory of a taste, avoiding recognition.

the echo of every thing,
the gold of Coltrane, single notes radiating life
the theory of resurrection in an empty room
memory of shadows, becoming flesh.

Nothing
the theory of no thing,
color, taste drained from each moment
removing every molecule, atom, energy wave
creating a place where nothing can exist.

the echo of no thing,
a deep dark hole, the den of Goya's Saturn
devouring heads and sons, living bodies
creating a place where nothing can bleed.

Something
  The theory of some things,
    the subatomic weight, length, name, genus, category
    of items made obsolete by version nth meta-release,
    structures re-built from bloated destruction.

  The echo of some things,
    the subatomic hope, the name of the soul
    a thin silk thread, an invisible white spider
    rebuilding a structure from ashes of too high hopes.

TALK TO ME, LITTLE BOY

by Alessandro Manzetti

I never believed in miracles
but I'm here now, comfortably numb,
in this so little dark room
—your head dreaming—
with a bottle of Southern Comfort,
half in its glass prison, half inside me.
I'm a sort of ghost flavoured with apricot . . .
Yeah, it's a miracle
only you and me, again, after all this time.
I know you're here, somewhere,
Where are you, little boy?

I was only a big mouth shadow,
before entering here,
—your head reminding—
Death is like a spell, sometimes
like a sunset stuck between
too high and thorny branches or barbed wire.
But I haven't given up
praying every night, following your smell,
climbing the vertical walls of Underworld
and finally finding a little hole (your ear)
to say these words,
Can you hear me?

I'm certainly not the Boogeyman . . .
look at me, I'm scared like a child.
I don't know where to put my feet
in this darkness, the nest of your thoughts
—your head awakening—
Help me, I see nothing but
this chilly room which looks like
a dance floor for dead things.
And you know, I love Coltrane's jazz,
the traffic noise, the sound of my fists
against the rubber face of frustration
—after I've been fired, on your planet—
Silence now could kill me, so . . .
talk to me, little boy.

But you're not really here . . . my son
—your head still made of flesh—
with all your familiar shouts and cries,
the bittersweet symphony of that night,
the syrup memory of my last day on Earth,
the last time I used my belt on your back
before the car crash, and the long way to my black
harbour.
You're no longer here . . .
—your head clear and turned on—
you forgot me, covering my face with a scribble
turning my voice into a fly buzzing.

What's left of me, here?
I'm nothing but a remote trace, a smell
of some old-fashioned aftershave,
an old blurry picture with a yellow sky,
waiting for the sun to die again,
with its sunset mechanisms repaired,
and to come back to my grave
without taking my belt off,
to convince you I existed,
like a good daddy, this time.

BLOOD STONE

by Linda D. Addison & Alessandro Manzetti

Inspired by Jill Bauman

Crushing each pebble of early life,
each person, place, thought, memory
even the secret, hidden, captured dreams,
all waiting in the bright shadows drinking
the path of fevered, motionless karma.

Crushing fresh-cut grass,
with little, young feet running fast
even risking to step on hornets,
or landmines of infinite wonders
exploding in millions of paths.

Catch & Release to find the lost souls
running in wild circles with nooses
tight around smiling necks, kicking to
resist, thrown to the ground, covered
in the sweat of whispered futures.

Catch & Release to follow the tail
of the beast of tomorrow's
continuously drifting, whipping yellow days
while blue dreams are collected, hidden
into rows of cans under too short beds.

Aggressive visions of classic healing
require Heliotrope, the Sun Stone, held
in a bleeding fist, invoking magical ways
known to the temporal lobe, not spoken but
tasted on the tongue, the grittiness of beauty.

Reddish visions of handprints
upon cave walls, the timeless shell of beauty,
without mirrors pretending to show your face
during the Big Bang of yourself,
millions of stone fragmented, everywhere.

More than a talisman, the crushed remains mix
with drops of blood to protect future generations
from perceived battles, wild lightning, conjured
guilt. Translucent strength stimulates latent clarity.
There is always a way to reject transformation.
More than a warning, a rosary of teeth
talks about a time without time
an unnamed day, dressed with a silver armor
reflecting bullets, uniform, the green ghost of uranium
and a flower in a dead mouth—the rejected apocalypse.

MARDI GRAS

by Alessandro Manzetti

I call her Mardi Gras
because she's a parade
(in purple, green and gold)
of all I ever wanted,
and dresses the flesh mask
of Ingres' lying odalisque,
with eyes survived—intact,
to the slow death of colors.
(mesmerized by an undead glance)

I call her in that way
because she's the French Quarter
of a grey city living inside me,
with her colonial beauty
with those lines, those curves
the spicy, voluptuous proportions
of her body, of toes barely touched
by Mississippi and Caribbean Sea;
(a Déjà vu of Baudelaire's Creole Muse)
something blended by different races,
by many harbors and oceans.
I call her Mardi Gras
because I saw her between hundreds of bodies
of a dancing procession, her nipples shining,
the next day, a raining day,
saw her again on the edge of a suburban street

lighting a fire, showing herself
to strangers, under an unknown oval moon,
her mouth sad, the red tongue long
as the Goddess Kali,
a wad of dollars tucked into golden tighty whities.

Since that day Mardi Gras is always with me
in the basement of my house
watching constantly the rotten ceiling,
sweating colors on the floor
(purple, green and gold pools of her)
screaming, day and night
frightening my dog and my
so impossible hope (*Why does it feel so strange?*)
to convince her to begin to change
into a miniature North Star,
to be owned by only one.

WHEN YOU FORGET ME

by Linda D. Addison

Inspired by *If You Forget Me* by Pablo Neruda

You think you know
all things.

But this is how it is:
when I look
at the blood moon, at the red streaks
of the slow cuts at my wrists,
when I touch
the candle's flame
the building soot
or the bloated blisters of my hands,
nothing carries you to me,
as if nothing exists,
odors, flowers, letters
became little memories
that sail
away from the world I no longer want.

Well, yesterday,
when little by little you stopped loving me
I shall love you more and more.

When suddenly
you forgot me,
did not look for me,
I began to stop feeling all things.

If you think me broken and mad,
the thoughts of pain
that became my life,
and you decide
to let me drown off the shore
of my shattered heart, without roots,
remember
back on this last day,
on this last hour,
I shall lift my bleeding wrists
and my mind will sail away
to seek sweet death.

But
if after the last day,
the last hour,
you remember you and I
without bitter deception,
if each night a shadow
climbs on your bed, to your lips,
ah my love, my torture,
in the flames of hell rebuffed,
in the nothingness I reside,
my love will feed on you, beloved,
and as long as you live, I will be in your dreams
never leaving you.

THE YELLOW HOUSE

by Linda D. Addison & Alessandro Manzetti

The Dutchman is painting his house
in chrome yellow, like the sun,
like the golden teeth of an archangel.
A bell rings, in the distance,
the holy scent of candied fruit
is floating all around.
No, she can't find me here, thinks the man,
—so far from Paris, and its demons.

The Dutchman is painting himself,
on the walls of the Yellow House,
sunflower's petals bloom from his head.
The light of Provence, in a moment,
walks in the window; a glimpse on the canvas,
then through an empty glass, becoming
a memory of the transparent red of wine.
Not a place of broken things, thinks the man
—so far from Paris, and its screams.

Evening, stars, and revelations.
What is the Dutchman afraid of?
Eternity. He can feel it on his skin,
sucking days like a cold leech.
That limitless space, he can't paint it all,
too much shadow, too much to take.
Someone knocks on the door, repeating

the same words: *Vincent.*
You again, thinks the man,
crawling under the table,
—she's waiting outside, pregnant.

The Dutchman found a path to the next
world in the walls of the Yellow House,
like the first memory of a dream, bright
still life captured by imperfect human
hands, fighting isolation, weeks ago he
found her in the field. And now: *Vincent.*
Not you again, whispers the man,
squeezing his eyes closed, hands over ears,
—still she waits, refusing to leave.

The Dutchman found a road away from
the roaring city, from the broken. Why
are they afraid of him? *Alchemy.* He can
feel it under his skin, humming in each breath
like a newborn, suckling ideas from his noisy
brain. She knocks again. *Please*, he prays,
pressing his forehead against the rough wood floor,
—in his memory, her face is bright yellow.

Daffodils cover every inch of her skin,
obscuring the details of her face. Blue irises
seep from her fingertips. The knocking stops,
an echo of pleading rings in his ears. Was
this a dream, left by the moans of crowded
buildings, of their need to change him,
—in his memory, their faces are blurred gray.

They: faceless, would-be teachers, with
hands frozen in muted palettes. He crawls
from under the table. She was never there,
his ears deceived him. The cracks in the
walls began to weep. *I will give you color,*
—I will give you stars, and revelations.

TIMEKEEPERS OF ANGKOR WAT

by Linda D. Addison

The green canopy of the forest, host trunks in the grip
   of charismatic strangler fig trees, watch quietly,
   as the sun dips behind the spires of temple walls,
   one young monk, kneeling among the crumbling
   sandstone carvings of deities and dancing girls,
   lights another incense, closes his eyes, chants,
   ignoring the setting sun, warnings of his teachers.

The coming full moon eclipse reminds monkeys, bats,
   and most humans to avoid figs & devotionals this
   night, when the Timekeepers roots break free of
   space/time, strangler trees loosen the death grip on
   host trunks, bone-colored serpentine roots stretch &
   jerk in the air, reenacting 850 year old memories of
   worshippers and robbers, love and violence.

The faithful know to stay outside the boundaries on
   this night, leaving the job of maintaining the
   crumbling walls to longer living life forms than
   humans, and when visiting to whisper, leaving
   only thoughts of peace within the temples, not
   to add ferocity to structures protected & supported
   by the multi-limbed silent assassins, who seek
      fast retribution on this night.

The young monk hears a strange scraping, opens his
eyes, sees in the dimming light a trick(?) of vision,
the flesh-colored root of the strangler tree shaped
like a non-human limb rolling back & forth, lifting
from the ground. He scrambles back into the waiting
arms of a lattice of roots, trembling on the decaying
carvings of Vishnu. The roots tightly swaddle him.

Oriented to the west by the unbreakable embrace of the
strangler roots, the bas-relief's carvings pressing
against his back, the young monk looks up at the
apsara & devatas adorning the opposite wall, all
memories of lessons, life becomes one short breath,
roots melt into his skin/soul/Self dissolves into every
thing-ness, no time to mourn/rejoice the Becoming.

The morning/mourning brings quiet, strangler trees
return
to the slow dance of survival, transcending back to
Being, encompassing the broken bliss of purposeless
reality without judgement. When humans return to the
temple in the morning light, no one notices the new
painting, dancing with the devatas on the degrading
sandstone, a young being with three faces smiling . . .

INSIDE MY BELLY

by Alessandro Manzetti

Partly inspired by *Psalm IV* by Allen Ginsberg, 1960

Now I'll tell you my secret vision:
the impossible sight of her face,
—June, fabulous blooming thought—
They believe she can be found in heaven
or in a room upstairs of consciousness.
—Furnace, Voice, Beatnik Jazz—
It was no dream, I lay waking
on a red couch in my imaginary Harlem
—a middle-class apartment, I'm not a true poet—
having masturbated for no love,
having heard *The Lamb lies down on Broadway*
—A Lamb? I didn't get any of that—
and read half naked an open book on my lap.

I was thoughtless and turned a page and gazed
her face instantly appeared from a white hole
then disappeared,
—It's you in there, isn't it?—
and heard a voice, it was Henry Miller,
reciting something from the crapper of Purgatory
—With his twin angels June and Mara—
wearing his rosy robe and a dented halo.
The voice rose out of the page
'A prisoner has no sex. He is God's own private eunuch'

digging a finger inside my belly,
—Don't touch me!—
painting the wall with my vision,
my blood and my yellow hope:

She, with a star instead of her head,
on the balcony, here,
breathing my fake Harlem,
still alive, still so beauty, still June.
Red walls of buildings flashed outside,
in front of her, endless sky sad Eternity
breaks through buildings and each brick
of the same day, two years ago, still now,
when she decided to leave
flying on the sidewalk, down there
like an unlicensed angel.
'Please, forget me.'
She wept and held me in her dead arms
'Please, don't make me die every day.'
A whisper, her face changes,
—She, a sunflower in her mouth—
letting me walk, like a solstice
on the last mile of Tropic of Cancer.

Bang. Her face upon the tomb,
—Furnace, Sorrow, the Tchaikovsky's Pathétique—
a creaky gate, a big man, dressed like a gardener,
his gravedigger's deep voice:
"We're closing now, sir."

THE VICTOR (RE) WRITES THE HISTORY

by Linda D. Addison & Alessandro Manzetti

Non-engagement forced the minds
of those in charge, their orders
misinterpreted: getting the truth
wasn't the same as torturing proclaimed
innocence, many witnesses disappeared,
listed as runaways, no blame assigned.

   that's what was (re)written

Proof was gathered with the Time Machine,
overlooking the choice of Past(s), no one
mentioned selection of time supporting
the documented Present, they didn't want
to cease to exist, not that others had been
erased, that was forbidden by law.

   that's what was (re)written

Time Machine is a new model of meat grinder
that turns the pulp, the muscles of history
into white tasteless meatballs (altar breads);
chewing them, you won't find a trace
of perpetrators' juice, or a clove oil drop of regret.
It's a trick, like ground that hides the dead
or a witness without tongue and home.

that's what was minced, and eaten (by all)

Truth is vacuum-wrapped, frozen,
like a codfish observing its own death
for too long, through its rubber eyes,
while planets explode, and a new King
reads the whole story on the pearly skin
of an odalisque made of flesh and pixels (technocracy)
behind the armored door of his living Library.

that's what was forbidden to read (to all)

FAILED LOVE LESSONS

by Linda D. Addison

This is not my breath, it is yours, the false start,
    mis-aligned emotions sliding past the cut in
    your chest. That is not my opening revealing
    all secrets, it is yours, it used to be our hearts
        beating together.

This is not my hand, it is yours that caressed my
    face, breath quickening as the cut at your
    wrist released it, lies written in sleepy
    moments seeping out, crimson script,
        patterns of mis-used affection.

These are not my eyes, they are yours, can you
    finally see me, the real me, now that I have
    freed them from your confusing need to control.
    I suspect the tears of blood on your cheeks
        contain some truth.

It is not my skin, it is yours peeled away to allow the
    history of pain to write itself in the veins
    underneath, a map from the past to unseen future.
    There, there now, admitting wrong is no sin,
        hiding it is . . .

These are not my muffled cries, they are yours,
   denying, pleading for redemption I can not give,
   only seek out the truth of your abuse, interpreted
   through the echoes of devotional song, here in
   distant woods where you first seduced me.

This is my recovery, my need to understand how
   false love came to be, so I will know better
   next time, so I can learn . . .

NOTHING'S SACRED HERE

by Alessandro Manzetti

The man dressed in black
wears a strange necklace
a kind of rosary made of candy
with a little crucifix
hanging, shining.
His home is large as a cathedral
with multicolored oval windows
—gothic rosettes with weird scenes—
ancient traps for sun rays,
in that place where no star would enter.
His landlord is a blind old gentleman
with a beard so long
you can use it as a rope
to climb to Heaven.

The man dressed in black
often talks about Jerusalem,
angels, creatures made of fire.
But, in the evening, his mind runs
over the himself Hill,
where he buried young rainbows,
to say goodnight to them,
celebrating forced orgiastic destinies
with his Byzantine, so white face
that stands out among the gorgeous vegetations
of an upside-down Eden,

his well maintained garden of one hectare
which smells of incense,
full of carnivorous plants.

The man dressed in black
tells fascinating stories to big eyed little boys
—Twenty Thousand Leagues Under the Sea—
inside an out of sight room, with double bed
—A Journey to the Center of the Earth—
a place he calls 'the secret land of the braves'
where books, gods and young and old flesh
—The Kamasutra of the Angels—
meet together, for the first time,
inside a double bed
under rough red sheets.

ABOUT THE AUTHORS

LINDA D. ADDISON is an award-winning author of several collections, including *How To Recognize A Demon Has Become Your Friend*, and the first African-American recipient of the HWA Bram Stoker Award®. In 2018, she received the HWA Lifetime Achievement Award. She has published over 300 poems, stories and articles and is a member of CITH, HWA, SFWA and SFPA. Addison is a co-editor (with Kinitra Brooks PhD and Susana Morris PhD) of *Sycorax's Daughters* (2017), an anthology of horror fiction/poetry by African-American women. Catch her work in anthologies *Dark Voices* (2018), *Cosmic Underground* (2018), *Scary Out There* (2016), *The Beauty of Death* (2016). Website: www.lindaaddisonpoet.com.

ALESSANDRO MANZETTI is a Bram Stoker Award-winning author (and 7-time nominee) and editor of more than twenty five books in English and Italian, including works of fiction, poetry, and nonfiction. Among his works in English: the novels *Naraka* (2018) and *Shanti* (2019), the collection *The Garden of Delight* (2017), the poetry collections *Venus Intervention* (2015, with Corrine De Winter), *Sacrificial Nights* (2016, with Bruce Boston), *No Mercy* (2017) and *WAR* (2018, with Marge Simon). He edited the anthologies *The Beauty of Death Vol. 1*, (2016), *The Beauty of Death Vol. 2* (2017, with Jodi Renee Lester) and *Monsters of Any Kind* (2018, with Daniele Bonfanti). Website: www.battiago.com

THE END?

Not quite . . .

Dive into more Poetry Collections:

WAR by Alessandro Manzetti and Marge Simon
Brief Encounters with My Third Eye by Bruce Boston
No Mercy: Dark Poems by Alessandro Manzetti
Eden Underground: Poetry of Darkness by Alessandro Manzetti

Or other Tales from the Darkest Depths:

Novels:
The Mourner's Cradle: A Widow's Journey by Tommy B. Smith
House of Sighs (with sequel novella) by Aaron Dries
The Third Twin: A Dark Psychological Thriller by Darren Speegle
Aletheia: A Supernatural Thriller by J.S. Breukelaar
Blackwater Val by William Gorman
Pretty Little Dead Girls: A Novel of Murder and Whimsy by Mercedes M. Yardley

Novellas:
A Season in Hell by Kenneth W. Cain
Quiet Places: A Novella of Cosmic Folk Horror by Jasper Bark
The Final Reconciliation by Todd Keisling
Devourer of Souls by Kevin Lucia

Anthologies:
Tales from The Lake Vol.5, edited by Kenneth W. Cain
Fantastic Tales of Terror: History's Darkest Secrets, edited by Eugene Johnson
Welcome to The Show, edited by Doug Murano and Matt Hayward

Lost Highways: Dark Fictions From the Road, edited by
D. Alexander Ward
Behold! Oddities, Curiosities and Undefinable Wonders,
edited by Doug Murano
Gutted: Beautiful Horror Stories, edited by Doug Murano
and D. Alexander Ward

Short story collections:
Book Haven and Other Curiosities by Mark Allan Gunnells
Dead Reckoning and Other Stories by Dino Parenti
Frozen Shadows and Other Chilling Stories by Gene
O'Neill
Varying Distances by Darren Speegle
The Ghost Club: Newly Found Tales of Victorian Terror by
William Meikle
Ugly Little Things: Collected Horrors by Todd Keisling
Whispered Echoes by Paul F. Olson
Visions of the Mutant Rain Forest, by Bruce Boston and
Robert Frazier

**If you've ever thought of becoming an author,
we'd also like to recommend these non-fiction
titles:**

It's Alive: Bringing Your Nightmares to Life, edited by
Eugene Johnson and Joe Mynhardt
The Dead Stage: The Journey from Page to Stage by Dan
Weatherer
*Where Nightmares Come From: The Art of Storytelling in
the Horror Genre*, edited by Joe Mynhardt and Eugene
Johnson
Horror 101: The Way Forward, edited by Joe Mynhardt
and Emma Audsley
Horror 201: The Silver Scream Vol.1 and *Vol.2*, edited by
Joe Mynhardt and Emma Audsley
*Modern Mythmakers: 35 interviews with Horror and
Science Fiction Writers and Filmmakers* by Michael
McCarty

Writers On Writing: An Author's Guide Volumes 1,2,3, and 4, edited by Joe Mynhardt. Now also available in a Kindle and paperback omnibus.

Or check out other Crystal Lake Publishing books for more Tales from the Darkest Depths.

Hi readers,

It makes our day to know you reached the end of our book. Thank you so much. This is why we do what we do every single day.

Whether you found the book good or great, we'd love to hear what you thought. Please take a moment to leave a review on Amazon, Goodreads, or anywhere else readers visit. Reviews go a long way to helping a book sell, and will help us to continue publishing quality books. You can also share a photo of yourself holding this book with the hashtag #IGotMyCLPBook!

Thank you again for taking the time to journey with Crystal Lake Publishing.

We are also on . . .

Website:
www.crystallakepub.com

Be sure to sign up for our newsletter and receive three eBooks for free: http://eepurl.com/xfuKP

Books:
http://www.crystallakepub.com/book-table/

Twitter:
https://twitter.com/crystallakepub

Facebook:
https://www.facebook.com/Crystallakepublishing/

Instagram:
https://www.instagram.com/crystal_lake_publishing/

Patreon:
https://www.patreon.com/CLP

Or check out other Crystal Lake Publishing books for more Tales from the Darkest Depths. You can also subscribe to Crystal Lake Classics (http://eepurl.com/dn-1Q9), where you'll receive fortnightly info on all our books, starting all the way back at the beginning, with personal notes on every release. Or follow us on Patreon (https://www.patreon.com/CLP) for behind the scenes access, bonus short stories, polls, interviews, and if you're interested, author support.

With unmatched success since 2012, Crystal Lake Publishing has quickly become one of the world's leading indie publishers of Mystery, Thriller, and Suspense books with a Dark Fiction edge.

Crystal Lake Publishing puts integrity, honor, and respect at the forefront of our operations.

We strive for each book and outreach program that's launched to not only entertain and touch or comment on issues that affect our readers, but also to strengthen and support the Dark Fiction field and its authors.

Not only do we publish authors who are legends in the field and as hardworking as us, but we look for men and women who care about their readers and fellow human beings. We only publish the very best Dark Fiction, and look forward to launching many new careers.

We strive to know each and every one of our readers while building personal relationships with our authors, reviewers, bloggers, podcasters, bookstores, and libraries.

Crystal Lake Publishing is and will always be a beacon of what passion and dedication, combined with overwhelming teamwork and respect, can accomplish: unique fiction you can't find anywhere else.

We do not just publish books, we present you worlds within your world, doors within your mind from talented authors who sacrifice so much for a moment of your time.

This is what we believe in. What we stand for. This will be be our legacy.

Welcome to Crystal Lake Publishing—Tales from the Darkest Depths

CPSIA information can be obtained
at www.ICGtesting.com
Printed in the USA
LVHW080512121020
668563LV00008B/237

9 781646 338573